under
the aegis
of a
winged mind

under the aegis of a winged mind

makalani bandele

Winner of the 2019
Autumn House Poetry Prize

AUTUMN
HOUSE PRESS

PITTSBURGH, PA

Autumn House Press receives state arts funding support through a grant from the Pennsylvania Council on the Arts, a state agency funded by the Commonwealth of Pennsylvania, and the National Endowment for the Arts, a federal agency.

author photo: Andre Howard
cover photo/art: Jo Mackby, adapted from the series *Hoarder House*, 2019

ISBN: 978-1-938769-58-0
Library of Congress Control Number: 2020937202

Sea to sea, America in 1945 was as backward a country musically as it was racially. Those of us who tried to push it forward had to suffer...

DIZZY GILLESPIE

to the ones that make it all possible:
nef, natalie, elijah, cohen, makaila, and cheikh.

table of contents

bebop convention

3 - blues in b for charlie
4 - the sound of thinking about distant objects
5 - quick recipe for genius
6 - mary lou williams's piano workshop (after fred moten)
8 - earl of harlem meets the high priest of bebop (alternate take)
10 - ghost of the piano
11 - cutting contest: earl of harlem vs. art tatum (for who buys the next pitcher of pabst)
12 - gigan: the cruel blues
13 - coping
14 - earl of harlem meets the high priest of bebop
15 - leit[blue]motif
16 - earl of harlem swear he in love with the little piano girl of east liberty
17 - cutting contest: earl of harlem vs. art tatum (for who buys the next pitcher of pabst) (lost
       live recording)
18 - piano ode to the cabaret card

when you bug out

23 - riff on g7 (after thelonious monk's "in walked bud")
24 - mad man at the finger palace
26 - mad man at the finger palace (alternate take)
27 - after ect
28 - tune as an asylum
29 - scary meds
30 - what to do while fresh ideas are organizing
31 - earl of harlem in his simplest form, a poor man's diagnosis
32 - earl of harlem swear he in love with the little piano girl of east liberty (bud's take)
33 - pianism
36 - pearl of harlem
38 - pianism (alternate take)

suite 120 études

41 - étude op. 8, no. 7
42 - étude op. 8, no. 2
43 - étude op. 8, no. 6
44 - étude op. 8, no. 4
45 - étude op. 11, no. 5
46 - étude op. 11, no. 11
48 - étude op. 15, no. 1
49 - étude op. 15, no. 3

un poco loco

53 - mnemonic fragments (ballad for crossing the unbridgeable chasm)
55 - piano solitaire
56 - earl of harlem at the golden shovel
57 - the negro section as frontage
58 - 12-bar F blues with a few substitutions thrown in
59 - wor studios, new york city, may 1, 1951
60 - tempus fugue-it
61 - earl of harlem swear he in love with the little piano girl of east liberty (alternate take)
62 - last supper of bop
64 - mingus of the ninth circle
66 - the portrait of an artist in his daughter's aural imagination
67 - crash
68 - homegoing and repass
70 - solo

paris spring, autumn in new york

73 - lost in the 8th arrondissement
75 - earl of harlem on bob thompson's garden of music
76 - dissipation: a bop
77 - off night: a piano trio
78 - last call
80 - fraternité
81 - aubade: earl of harlem composing extemporaneously
83 - gigan: epistle to neptune
84 - blue heron
85 - celia

appendix

91 - notes
95 - acknowledgments

bebop convention

"Every time a cop hits a Negro with his billy club, that old club says, 'BOP! BOP!...BE-BOP!'....That's where Be-Bop came from, beaten right out of some Negro's head into them horns and saxophones and piano keys that plays it...That's why real Bop is mad, wild, frantic, crazy—and not to be dug unless you've seen dark days, too."

JESSE B. SEMPLE *(Langston Hughes's fictional, quintessential Harlem resident)*

blues in b for charlie

éclat of eighth notes,	your otherwise	known
as heft in gauge you're	ear-minded, a felon of	time-
divided current—deft	measures (twice), cut	the clothes off bob johnson once.
gathered down by music's	edge—your wakes	break
blues up and down, and side- except the locution is electric	ways at the same time; blue	outthrust dulcetly—lester-like, to amaranthine.

the sound of thinking about distant objects

                                                    makes a pretty irony somewhere where
the notes can find some rest,
an octave over, seventh interval
on the up, major seventh

                              on the down: what happens when you make it scream
                         like calvin from up the street in the back of a paddy wagon?
                              sweat up and down, old white lady calling the police
cursing the other directions, they go in—
that's so fascinating in the way the black self is this way.
follow monk, elmo, and al all the way,

                                        out the open intervallic, humming
                                        it down bona fide back alleyway
                                        behind al's tv repair bop.

the boys run around the yard,
swearing they black and hip.
bud aint showing nobody shit,
just listen. in so many notes telling them
they don't have to play so loud.

                                        play loose.

quick recipe for genius

take a feeling
black people aint really felt in 600 years,

say freedom,
but sing liberty.

take mama's big brown eyes,
and curio with intersectional.

pour in half
piano and half amazing.

the tchaikovsky is for thickness.

take it all in.

sprinkle a lil sumthin sumthin
of sumthin mad
peculiar on top. chill

and indefatigably stare.
if you like, you

can add a fresh sprig of
technique for garnish, to make white
folks more confused
about their humanity.

mary lou williams's piano workshop (after fred moten)

"There is, then, a real and special influence of woman."
—Anna Julia Cooper, *Voice from the South*

where you brought new ideas if you

were thinking them. a woman's place

is in her heart and fingers, rolling
through intervals of instantaneous opus

like sardonic eyes tired of the excuses. no kitten
on the keys, she like the way she ditty bop.

her cut of acute ear like cloud framed

in window all late night. the way the

conversation went array and early into

the afternoon the next day. baby, y'alls'
chords is screwy and need a screwdriver

from her manufacture. so mary ate a music

school. hits 'n' bits from the tips like a

teacher getting her lessons together in

a vase of bright yellow begonias. chicken frying,
pot of aughts on the stove. only the coldest cold

water cornbread. their uninvited, open invitation
to come up to hers like an upper room. like an
advent, their arriving with voyage in sound

metamorphosis. everybody on the white shag

carpet continued with one accord in

experimentation, and prolific phraseology

was reconnaissance. enrolled in her

suppositious search for her interior

paramour. what freedom of movement,
what to be moving felt like chord to chord,

kinston to st. albans, eighth avenue express,
where she was going, wasn't there before

she left, she made it up as she went along.

yet, it's quite another thing to carry a stave
around with you wherever you go.

from her flat was launched a thousand styles.

earl of harlem meets the high priest of bebop (alternate take)

dig that hat
rakishly tilted to
the bank. you, the cat with
          them hats, scooch

over some. put
your bailey on and play awhile.

all hat and
          expert   prelude makes
you deadly,   felonious mob as art
music. is you

                   is or is
you aint? a bowler full of

          many minds decorating
space with time.

snuck a half-pint   of whiskey in
          here under this
fez. hat trick.

asian conical hat tricks you into
                   thinking you're jungle

                   and grown enough
          to slick mouth gee-gee. but it
                   also could've been
          that whiskey. now,

where can i find   an unpredictable
                   helmet across pinnacle?
                   or a temple
of fedora with upshot uptown? that
   your herringbone trilby
                          i swiped in
the foyer? my   bad. but that
brim was stingy
as a club
owner, but not as crooked as
a record label.
                   felt hat versus

cops' batons, who   you think won

                        that one? that's

            one cap my
skull could never. of porkpie hat's
angry drunk. hat

as hopefully not
            too much dark   hope cooking in

a spoon in

a nook down
the hallway from   lucretia's cold water
                        flat where rent
            party   people dance

                        the ceiling for lack of room
on the floor.
can i have
            some   of that sombrero? can i
borrow that ironclad
                yarmulke that escaped
from labor camp? can i hold

your   bamboo hat

                for a lark?
            do i play too fast in
this beret with
a piano pin?

urbane lid   says scores about a
                man of few
            words like chords.
            that cat is a distant hat
for miles of
            nothing but arpeggios.
bruh,
the newsboy cap says it all.

ghost of the piano

they said for the sake of the insurance money that jazz was dead, that the poor chile's wails waking them in the middle of the night was not a baroque, left-handed figure. the penthouse and everything in it were señorita's inheritance from a murderer and rapist, like other captains of industry that's how he'd acquired something to pass down. his portrait in a khaki field uniform and black leather jackboots hung above the petite rodin and menaced ada till the end of her days. the first time she saw it, she could not find the notes to sing for a month of sundays. when ada started working for señorita, the piano would suddenly and inexplicably break out into dvořák's humoresque in the middle of tiger rag, as if, by god, god was playing and not this apparition of a fat black man. one fat tuesday, willie the lion pushed the damned thing out the twenty-fifth-floor cathedral window after random keys played dead and broke his stride. the ground below became an embittered coral sea of shards and pieces of mostly stained glass, mahogany, steel wire, iron, felt, various other woods, and metals. skinny-legged, little brown-skinned girls danced around the kaleidoscopic catastrophe and picked up the tiniest colors and ate them or saved them to make bracelets. the family heirloom lay there for days in hundreds of pieces but still warbled at night— eventually they scrapped the metal and burned the remains and all its august hammers. the soul of art tatum's fingers fled in the heavy sustain of smoke. the ashes were used to fertilize the hydrangea, peonies, and jasmine. the air in the courtyard, even to this day, smells a bit of stale pabst blue ribbon.

cutting contest: earl of harlem vs. art tatum (for who buys the next pitcher of pabst)

a licked right index finger in the air,
as if to test the atmosphere for swing.

chord-contorted fingers strike the keys: background thunder.
piercing wonder.

      welcome to the palace of fingers so fascinating.
      metacarpals meet your maker, god is in the house, got the whole world in his
hands, and he aint taking no skimpy nickel bags.

dash of meta-

carpals. a little impromptu odyssey
of digits.
      didn't you hear? all the guys and gals are fingertips because there is a chance,
however slight, to kiss lucy.
      fingers as selves entertaining what spray of violets might burst forth from the
piano.
a figment of fingers. all kinds of crazy phalanges   tearing up the nuthouse together.
everybody under the sound of phalanges, left ones colder but the right more smoothly,
and the sheer velocity of their thinking together.   then, somebody got on an insane
roll of thirty straight rolls of nine finger chords the hard way.

rows and rows of unfurling ease   on around the corner, bud shoots up
and nods in later.

right when the mind is a piano body best embodied in the fingers, bud got the little bitty
babies in his fingers.

sympathies as an array of feelers, over and over, in tight succession.
greasy fingers and their diamond tips.

      somebody's finger wave gleams.
          how   ever does art   attain and then maintain
that euphoric quality   of drunkenness
in the fingertips?

a sip with every finger but the pinky. a tea for two thousand fingers. could have sworn
you heard the fingertips say, *the anarchist's wife is the real anarchist.*

gigan: the cruel blues

after-hours with six hands up in uptown.
put the *ooh op knot* on that bean as if

you didn't know already the cops are crueler in philly.
at the third station of the rail crossing, swallowing
blood, crying out, *my head is not a keyboard—*

to pound out phrases with elbows and forearms
off the offbeat till a side of the face dents in.

four minutes before midnight and not a cloud in the
sky, they are all a swelling around the brain. this little lamb

lost his head and never found shelter for his notions again.
the hem up hours after at the precinct was

grisly punctuation: flying knees and fists blur into a colored
lightshow from a busted eardrum. would it be possible
to do another take of "america the beautiful" upside your head?

the swollen eye throbbing can't stop restating the melody.
the sound guy thinks your pain sounded good.

coping

it wasn't anything so laboratory he was doing
listening to his cooler selves to see if he could find modal ways
to live in the negation.

                                        the walls climbing
while he's climbing the walls.
vials, hoses, and spoons hidden in crevices you find looking for you. a little blood and a little
death in a syringe. bunch shouldered, hunched over. every shut eye aint somewhere asleep
under a torn awning you tell yourself, so you don't jump off the bridge.

he and lambent aster's hotshot got to talking,
foaming a little at the mouth.

contrary to some good sock it to me,
all that running up and down the street just proved crises are gigs, too. you gotta dope to
curl. and curling around is like when you stumble on the bus for free and still demand a
transfer.

amen, brotha.

fifteen cycles of institution per second does your whole head in in back to backs in two dif-
ferent studio cities. keeps your days and nights off minor.

corner of your head sharp like a homburg, sharp like it's just easier to swank. is you is or is you aint? all hats off. hat off its tip. tip top hat. a little tip of the hat. all cap and action, what a composition. ushanka as an homage to stravinsky's *the rite of spring*. that duckbill is kosher, *thou shall not abide pigs*. if a nig-mane only had a bulletproof boater to breathe against. beanie bad as a good whuppin. got a *black-and-tan fantasy* with a pith helmet in the plaza. aviator cap with goggles that see what's what, and if it's shonuff. bebop cap. curated bowler having a nervous breakdown. at lucretia's last rent party,   get that guy off the ceiling all in stride and pass the hat. odds are you can't tell me nothing under this stetson. therapeutic fez for your tuberculosis. mad bomber hat as required personal protective equipment for the state hospital. taciturn hat, brim smaller, crown taller for your conjurer. keep it under your kufi. that hat is a cat all around town. flat cap. high high hats. the long american songbook beneath the kangol. got a fez and no head. got a mother who's the pearl of harlem always coming to see me. if i'm jesus, and art is god, who's he?

leit[blue]motif

basie's curiosity carries him uptown to a backroom at clark monroe's and sits him with a neat glass of scotch in the curve of a grand piano monk is teaching to discover his ideas as he develops them. *duh-dun duh-dun duh-dun dun dun* basie is nonplussed, but never more in the house. monk's grandson-of-a-sharecropper hands, thick and immense as thunderheads with fingers splay, flatted as fifths across the keys—*duh doobie doobie doobie doobie dudn doobie do do*—like a flock of polyphonic birds lighting inquisitively from branch to branch in a great elm; they dare not frighten the neighboring finches from their nests. basie, not that he was sleep sleep, wakes up between the second and third heaven to what sounds to him like wind chimes sprinkling a random music in the backyard before a storm. *duh doobie doobie doobie doobie dudn doobie do do*

home is the goal of the game.
and monk is a home resplendent in memory,
the rhythm of partly sunny, atmospheric as the layered concoction of gases above the surface of the planet; his melodic lines—*duh-dun duh-dun duh-dun dun*—the decor of deeps of sky, the blue room of basie's childhood. all this whimsy and running around, the glee in the phrasing, reminds basie of when he was a kid back in jersey playing sandlot baseball in the open field beside his house. jump notes like morning glory espaliered along the fence that extends out between the empty lot and house. *william james basie, get your narrow tail in this house. it's starting to rain, and it's almost time for dinner. ah mama, i just hit a home run to tie the game. duh doobie doobie doobie doobie dudn doobie do do*

monk finishes his romp with a humph.
basie goes back to his blues less lonely, confident that it's light precipitation, scattered heartache, a tin ear for the complicated chords of rainfall.

earl of harlem swear he in love with the little piano girl of east liberty

love's seeing a woman how she sees herself,
and getting outta the goddamn way.
not you or any man could replace my art.
with your heartstrings in c minor. ease back lonely,

i'ma need you to stay outta my goddamn way.
with all your allemande inclinations to tear shit up
with heartstrings in c minor. ease back, lonely,
fool like you'd trade l'amour for cheap liquor.

i got my own inclinations to tear it up. and this
passion fires the chest differently than irish whiskey.
fool like you'd trade l'amour for cheap liquor.
funny valentine, have to laugh to keep from crying,

cuz passion fires a chest differently than irish whiskey.
go for broke, go get uncertified in sensible,
funny valentine. have to laugh to keep from crying.
love aint easy as shooting cold fire into your vein.

but hey, go for broke, go get uncertified in sensible.
you gonna learn passion is being invaded from inside,
love aint easy as shooting cold fire into your vein, and
even love couldn't drag me from my baldwin.

passion is being invaded from inside the inside.
this inner orchestra send me integrally to solo.
even love couldn't drag me from my baldwin,
you got to precede the paradigm that anticipates you.

my inner orchestra send me integrally to solo.
not you or any man could replace my art.
baby, i precedes paradigm that anticipates me.
love's seeing a woman how she sees herself.

cutting contest: earl of harlem vs. art tatum (for who buys the next pitcher of pabst) (lost live recording)

welcome to the palace of fingers

all you can hear is a figment of fingers so fast
a licked right index finger in the air
                        somebody's finger wave gleams with reveries
                        as if to test the atmosphere for swing

            metacarpals, meet your maker, god's in the house

he got the whole world in the splay of his fingers
                        like each finger is touching on each continent
like everyone's under the sound of phalanges
                        a little impromptu odyssey of digits

            a hundred-meter dash of metacarpals

didn't you hear? everybody's fingertips
                        because there is a slight chance to kiss lucy.
each feeler a deeply feeling vehicle
                        full on feelers in the rhythm of nonstop

            right when the mind's ear is a piano body

he got you and me and the lil' bitty babies
                        best embodied in the discreet math of fingers
            a euphoria of feelers breaks out

sympathies as an array of feelers
                        over and over in tight succession
sip with every finger but the pinky
                        a tea for two thousand fingertips

piano ode to the cabaret card

"Put down the knitting, the book and the broom
Time for a holiday, yes
Life is a cabaret, old chum
So come to the cabaret."
                              —Louis Armstrong, "Cabaret"

even if you loved the
piano and it loved you.
twenty weeks at the long viral in 1953
(at six nights per
week and four sets
per night) is knuckle-busting
with a bureau to raise
off top. the workhorse modern
soloist is the chattel
of 52nd street.

52nd street theme running all down
the side of his dome compliments of
a cop's blackjack.
cops looking for any excuse,
play the wrong note and they're ready
to break your fingers.
he knew better than to walk
down the street with that white woman,

but she loved that tempo
only he could enforce. couldn't change key with

him like his fine art required,
                    if you had all the hands in harlem.

                    turnbacks is fair play.
to be well acquainted with
a jail or two, a whole lot of
racket. a whole lot of people's
bread got messed up, a whole
lot of people's heads.

easy answers aren't cheap. the times a body can't handle its whole weight.
this tip jar of broken promises. check the fine print. sal's skimming off the top of the door.
the debt from a thousand people's cuts—
how you end up owing money after polishing all the corners?

　　　　　whenever the music stops, the many hangers around
　　　　　for all their smack,

and the huge puff of smoke
that billows out and up from you when
you can't stop dragging the
anchor. Great societies
don't starve their artists. in the grand
schema of cards, if you got to pay to play,
fuck a cabaret.

when you bug out

The constitution of madness as a mental illness, at the end of the eighteenth century, affords the evidence of a broken dialogue, posits the separation as already effected, and thrusts into oblivion all those stammered, imperfect words without fixed syntax in which the exchange between madness and reason was made. The language of psychiatry, which is a monologue of reason about madness, has been established only on the basis of such a silence.

MICHEL FOUCAULT

riff on g7 (after thelonious monk's "in walked bud")

game recognize this broke called, *aint got nobody* to love and care for me, as a

buzz feeling you feel all askew in the dislocated arc back. jump right in: *joshua fit*

da battle of jericho, quote, unquote. that space needed to arc, needed to, say,

get down behind the piano for shelter from all the violence going on. gimme a

breakneck, a beat down, a vehicle of triplets six ways from sunday. i know for

fact you caint nonfigurative this muthafucka of a nightstickin' them put on him head.

mad man at the finger palace

the first few days locked away
without a piano, are not like days
with nights, but like nights
with nights within nights,

where moon and stars
are painted over with triple coating of dull
dark blue. pajamas, scrubs,
and vicarious gowns abstract

and digress about in sashay,
so you go with your first mind.
the monotonous conference is
of recital.

all the hours you want
are locked and heavy. the staff's
sanitized hands, despite choke holds and payback
rabbit punches.

humming lights overhead if
you give them attention, and you just
as soon be distracted by droning
filament as you would meltdowns and inauspicious

monologues.   the presence of absence's
eerie eyes, a wild-angled neck straining
to look at you, the manifold affiliations
you can't seem to connect, but you can
sometimes direct when you can find a direction.

tell ya what, touch
me again out of   my connotation.

her sleepwalking   wherever she goes. how
the water looks and smells electric.   it's not right
what society has turned us into. everyone is saying
everyone is saying, *don't say piano-less, say, pills*
in a cup, please. even if it's not the truth or doesn't

make sense, say what they want. even the little jay
is quiet as an alternative to reason.

*hey malleus,
do you know where the notes stashed themselves?*

one night, a pair of socks in house shoes drags
a counter melody up and down the hallway
until the shift nurse reapplies restraints.

with that operations are ordered, high jinks
ensued, composition dazzled. next morning,
eighty-eight keys chalked on the day room wall:

*duh da duh da duh da da da da da   duda looda dudeit
duh da duh da duh da da da da da   duda looda dudeit
da da da duh da da da da duh da da   duda looda dudeit duda looda dudeit
duda looda dudeit duda looda dudeit*

if all day, every day you play a keyboard
you've drawn on the wall,   and get downright glottal with it,
it's clear to them
you belong here.   but practice makes the brain

feverish, frees the fingers,   and   the edges
of the edges extend   only as far as they can.

mad man at the finger palace (alternate take)

every damn time	signature— i can't feel	my ears in my fingers anymore,
as i put them to the piano	of dull wall to dream.	how every dissonance is just chalk.
did you hear that	midnight cloud bank	console a tear of moon in the mirror?
god was in the house,	i hear fats saying that	night, but the mirror
bursts with eighty-eight	quiet mélanges for the	memory trying to variate off it.
everyone is saying	everyone is saying, *you're*	*hearing things.* problem is, it's not scalar.

after ect

august came in with the rec room a killing floor.
the first day i painted the baby grand blue,
air soughed all around, an unrubbing

rubbed all wrong. a warbler in the poplar
woodshedding second branch from the
top, a flutter about debussy. leaves didn't catch

the light right, they didn't twist easily in the breeze.
a courtship loud and wild in the treetops.
forecasted bach inventions dead in the center

of a ring of dope fiends. i come here every day in notes
to self-adhesive. i looked out when they closed down
the ferry to the land of intervals, there was no glow

about her through her lithe insignia. hard to anticipate her
timing in time. she arouses in me: bouquet
of dead butterflies. at a place in my parabola, where every

instrument had its own room. my breathing played
with me. their charge and denials of discharge
chased all the clouds away that hide me from fulcrums.
the fewer voices in the voicings, simpler.

tune as an asylum

considering the draft from a revolving door of no return, we

had to open a small window to a real

 small world we can't recall like when clouds in the sky were cool

to the touch of reality—we
got a pot   to formulate in, but nowhere to germinate freely. left

home with a foretaste of the wildest horse, a drag like school
                                                    without music. ask the walls if we
                                    have sweet blood in a secret attic. the lurk
out of grasp of late.
blue eyes flit suspiciously back and forth, they know we

transpose keys off the doom, difficult for others to strike.

so mad i can't even see   straight

                          ahead in a corrugated room tilted and spinning from the side effects. we
are passengers on the lost train. the steel on steel sings up the tunnel. crossing the river is sin.

if you must, do it swiftly, definitively.   ear of lithium ringing. we

argue with the charts you can't argue with. the sun thin
and mean through the window like cheap gin

spit in your eyes, sitting on a dead man for disambiguation. we

have all the changes to talk to at times,   *why call it jazz,*

we didn't name your baby june?
                                                    i be damn sometimes if we

don't convulse with electricity and damn near die.
dreams of cutting everybody again, and it won't be too soon.

scary meds

the moon is an uncareful scythe out there. the negotiables reverted to non- and put some stank on themselves as detergent. interim of maestros got your hands around your throat

in the process. of pinpointing. jackpot blows up. there are several worlds for it: not found, lapse,

barely hemisphere,

technically. eyes like mean shades. cheek the fit pills.

and cancelled rows of faces' mouths cloud

in the process. *hello, mr. powell, are you in there?*

                not really sure. anapestic larynx,

      din of disjuncture, derangement is

           a whirring, oscillating

           ache of every little inkling framelessly.

                            technically,

they put you in a box for an instrument you'd never think

was inexpressible. days don't add up to real numbers, spending so much energy in conversations with your selves. then, the change event in many tabular forms, technically. what choices would you give up

for a piece of intuition, regularity, some affection? *reply to the question: where are you?*

takes forever

and ever in real-time drool.

wake up in the middle of the night with leg cramps

from the sixth hell. a handful of hair.

what to do while fresh ideas are organizing

my mother, pearl, with folded hands, in rooms patiently waiting. her hands are a shimmering flame. time is precious in the inspiration. her wriggling in the doctor's ear. a blanket for a shawl, taking three buses to the hospital in a blizzard to come get me. *how is he getting better, when he believes the wall is a piano? at least he plays a real one at home.* like the earnest search for the b section of a maple tree. not a figure yet, but the contours of one. *he's even composed pieces on and for shadows he sees, called "études for chalk piano and shadows on the wall." quite stunning, really.* the insistence that we be somebody somewhere impedes assembly. i'm in the middle of the piece with melody all around. pleasantries being extended between tulips. i honor the invitation to come into their reed study, convene a wily forum. mama takes me by hand and leads me to black with outside. the best improvisers are always listening way out ahead of you, they know what you need to hear, and play it so your toes never touch the ground. *mrs. powell, your son has difficulty keeping everything straight in his head.* but they just want me to telegraph my phrases to make it more convection. they will never know what it is like to be honest as dew before first light. keep your ears on swivel, be ready to move on general principle.

earl of harlem in his simplest form, a poor man's diagnosis

accompaniment often had difficulty
finding him.
she remembers thinking
to herself when he was very
young that something was different
about him. different eyes. oddness
that begged to differ. you heard rain,
he heard differently.
what for him wasn't going in every different
direction so fast he often couldn't keep it standard?
different ideas, strangely different.
difference done differently. a different seventeen
month span every seventeen months.
the notes were a different
distance in the mirror
he gazed in with
a different distant look
for hours after gigs. how
can even your calluses be different?
sadly, the different ways different
chemicals react differently in different bodies.
too many days and nights of different
cocktails of alcohol,
drugs. there is a difference
between eccentric and erratic, and unfortunately,
he often split it. cops didn't really treat him
differently, without even asking his name
or for identification they beat him
just to have something to laugh about later.
in the prospect of all this apparatus,
he was a difference engine.
he woke up broke every day in the middle
of a different bazaar,
from booth to booth, pushing his art.

earl of harlem swear he in love with the little piano girl of east liberty (bud's take)

circles of fifths in search of level
gots to soak in your own
no way home
up on sugar hill

you gots to soak in your own stuff sometimes
funny valentine, crying
up on sugar hill near 144th & st. nick
darling exigency

funny valentine, have to laugh to keep from crying
love's easy
darling exigency like entablature
slow your finger rolls against season of heartbreak

love's easy as shooting cold fire into my vein
a heart is an instrument of uncompromising pulse
slow your finger rolls
got a love jones

a heart is an instrument of uncompromising pulse
upright baldwin piano for a heart
got a love jones
love is the piano playing for your fingers

upright baldwin piano for a heart
nothing fires up chest like irish whiskey
love is the piano
fool like me'd trade l'amour for cheap liquor

nothing fires up chest like irish whiskey
with luxuriant withholding
fool like me'd trade l'amour for cheap
go for broke, go get

left holding with withholding
as if to catch ones breath unfaithful to the heart
go for broke, and go get uncertified in sensible
aint trying to hear it

as if to catch
no way home
lush days light hinge aint trying
circles of fifths in search

pianism

        called it in a key everybody can touch without fear
        of being institutionalized,   tempo

tipping its hat to the ladies at the bar, a full bar ahead, artifice to divert attention away from
some impotence.

       how a rain falls but the dirt is tougher. the new ground broke him as much as he
broke out
     of stethoscopes to subtly restate what was understated back to him.

       with friends you can usually skip the small talk
       and go straight to the outlying. take great care in
       your notes' criteria. it's insurgent to ask someone
       something where the answer is longer than
       the journey. that's why he transgresses

the bar lines a lot of the time, as if it were him chasing the police
screaming the other way down the street.
here come

an overshot bridge, an evening quilt
with a purview, and the bad landing (ended
up in a sundown town messing around
after sundown,
and lived to tell about it.
is that bad enough for you?). here come

a code laboratory
and its speculative force of self-
awareness tulips vis-à-vis ebonies and ivories.
some boogie as a site of protest.

you wouldn't think that he'd take
this opportunity right now to rest,
but every code laboratory has an
interstitial in the corner consisting of
rest.

around back were distinctly distant galleries, and an extension chamber he get vast in. later, when lyricism heightens and somebody pulls a knife over who was dancing with whom, you thought he was gone and not going to get back in time, but just then he substitutes a motivic arrival with substitution motifs, and it sounded like kismet; he had sewed the groove back, and there wasn't a seam.

you don't appreciate the way his head fits in this space?

stands to reason, then, the more dramatically ascending the freight elevator, the more you can't go backward and forward at the same time, but he can sure make it lilt like he is.

pearl of harlem

to not only reify the audacity to swing,
but on your mama
and to swell her eye all up out to here.

                              then, she like this in the air with that eye one time
                              and your wheels roll right out from under you.
this be about a bee bumping around a crocus's pistil
she loved.
this be about she
and her magnolia entourage
long-suffering all this tender-headedness.

them country ham sandwiches
wrapped in wax paper for the long road ahead. mama's

        boy's mama like a worried vignette. she got a mean moan in the vestibule with wide
applications. and oh, how she loved to do the st. vitus's day dance with you when it's
disruptive.

                              moreover, the move over
                              and let granny put her own hip back in place.
                              she didn't know sometimes how they was going to make it
                                          on that broken hip.
her did what she had to do. her cook a mean cultural

process in the morning for you
after getting you out of jail.

what do you do when the needle can't seem to find
the groove?

she trains them up in the way they should go,
and man do they go to
more gigs, the head, hell, the bottle, movies, the waldorf, overseas and back,
even with the police harassing them.

after the piano's had
                                        its spell, who gonna go
to jim brown's with geejee and get aunt rosetta some function(al)
tonality and a pack of kools?

pianism (alternate take)

at a tempo that chased the police down the street screaming.
the finesse with which he attacked the ebonies and ivories
in a key everybody can square with refusal to enclosure.

only the diggers take great care in some criteria.
they usually skip the small talk and go straight to the journey
in search of the soloist that is not one, but a baritone city.

when lyricism heightens over who was dancing with whom,
the bad landing was made better by transportive around it.
being in a key everybody can locate within undifferentiated corsage.

here come an overshot bridge, an evening quilt with a purview.
here come self-awareness tulips vis-à-vis ebonies and ivories.
here come roughshod riding virtuoso over ad hominem and nem.

breaking new ground that broke him as much as he broke out
of it, substituting a motivic arrival with substitution motifs
in a key that works well on a bad piano. as a kind of coda,
here come pearl, granny, sugar lumps, and richie with pat hands, all of 'em.

suite 120 études
(études for chalk piano and shadows on the wall)

It is always instructive to study even the lesser works of the masters.

DOUG RAMSEY

étude op. 8, no. 7 (eight piano voicings of a spider)

what do eight spindly radii and two long sharps climb about?

the engineering of tensile moments,
                                        first as guidelines.

                    synecdochic entanglement in

a fibrous mirror opera. to light upon

gathering of bevels just freshly edged and expansive—
            oh, thin light architecture as contraption.

                    some signal lines,

say, *all caught up in.*
silk wires vibrating
from struggle. paracritical
eyes wild and many hungry for diminuendo of wings.

                                    bulwarks cracked open,
                        sour apple strings, pathos's hint of.

étude op. 8, no. 2 (eight piano voicings of brutality)

skunky reefer with aspirin and whiskey chaser
all the way home to keep bearings from winding out.

little sips of johnnie walker red on down the nice cop's beat giggling.

the night is philly and full of pigs' whispers, razor promises—*no good nigger.*

remember april

bloodied and splayed across whole tone scales?
civil defense sirens blaring between your shoulders, batons

 test the mettle of your skull.

                              bits of face spilling onto the ground.
this dissonant vengeance of disfigured
                    shapes.
back slaps, bootkicks to the ribcage, spleen, pancreas,

and you piss yourself.

split-lipped, busted-eyed run

of as much blunt force head trauma
the laws can get away with.

étude op. 8, no. 6 (eight piano voicings of a straitjacket)

an elbowroom of bas-
relief elbows. criss-
cross applesauce of a
     white angled
bowl leaves the stank
of duck cloth in the
palate.

of the stanch
   of archived documents
and like the cling-clang
of getting pulled in two
discrete directions.
    the somebody's help
     you need in augural
            tears.
a chest compressed
 into a wedge of breath.

is the fear
an immobile subjective
abnormally depicted
in black
and the space around
left all white
surpassing the tips?

étude op. 8, no. 4 (eight piano voicings of horse)

feral equus
takes
                    to blood.

                                        year of white mare,
                            rye and vermouth with riders
                                            she trusts.

emerald in gait.

                                        nod untypically
                            with adante, reins of direction,
                                uneven, even juxtaposed.

                    wildest ever;
        so gently smoothed.

                                    how is this moon so super,
                        so easily in sagittarius, as if one being
                                with cloud it's riding?

that unknowingly mysterious
        soft—fecund auburn.

                                        some pannonica then,
                                flattens back cravings
                                    in full gallop away.

étude op. 11, no. 5 (on composing windows and their proclivities)

most nights his heart never touches a pillow, and for days his stomach will not squeeze even a morsel—to break the envelope, he answers himself in generativity that's uncheckable out the gate. the touch he wanted to stay in without touch is a crossing the horn was for channel. lavender accents (specters hear it all, self-referring, in blow her lilac, the quite crucible) and nothing less than the tempo's adventurous differential gear made him more emergent, made him rephrase himself: notes of field toward evening. without awakening, to observe her slim approach faintly from a ways away. how much is that voicing in the window? such a plethora of foray you feel it in your missing teeth. this steinway treed a block of green chords, catch wind in the not-too-distant rupture, if you'd be led by your ossicles to the slaughter. detail without context. wash your clinquant corners, despite everyone feeling particularly raw at the moment. how much is that window for figure to form out of merge?

in an effort to be more precise when he does things, effectively triangulated it with travel from and in another time (any and everywhere between four beats to the bar, unpacking it behind the ravine, an easy distance that's hard to resolve). didn't know who was coming with, left some sleek fervor to the arrival of the perceptibly expressive force of left hand.

étude op. 11, no. 11 (last piano voicings of a monarch)

hard to keep him on his throne,
how tight are the pins in the damper? nerves

raw as licks are rapacious, and lonely
hours between possessing all ears.

matter of fringe's hortative verve, tempo:
chimeric. incite keys to riot out. but if he won't come

down, don't call the fire people who will send
the police, because they barely come to his block

even when it's on fire. has a look in his pocket
that was through you and everything around

you, but what was actually seen was
for what it was somewhere else. heard that way,

too, a single note's muffled thump like lone gunshot
reporting in the backwoods at night.

seminar in still after echo. incognito
between sets, vinegar-bitten air was a walk

through a wall, a heavy dose, but also spoon-
cooking, blood drawn into barrel,

the plunge that loosens all holds, all cozy, friends don't let
friends, friends that are users and not friends.

nobody knows about the raucous all taut
and entertained, ears color-struck, these black tar apparitions,

fields of mauve and fluted caps, fields of nothingness,
withdrawn, withdrawal, and further withdrawal

from the grasp most people need to hold to.
how funky are his fits of lucidity? when

little sequences of consequences conference
there is subtle curling of the right hand slightly

as awareness come back more aware
of itself gliding along a light interrogative.

not unlike a monarch that knows to float
somewhere it's never been,

arrive eager, predisposed, only then knowing
this was the destination all along.

étude op. 15, no. 1 (in liminal space between objective and subjective pianistic expression)

as parameter would have it,
he got
                    friends in high places keeping him high.
he keep an improvisational notebook
curled up with him,

sucking his thumb   in the fetal position
constantly revising in speculating.
they swear he sleep.

                                the lover
            is up on st. nick's striving.
            his jowl rest her hand in quaver.
is nostalgic a symptom, an asymptote for reaching
            into mismemory?
        she wants to crush he compose.
        woke up   in sky in his sleep with her.
        he couldn't if he tried.

babydoll, take us
on tour in that blue-sky lincoln.

 that launch is chirpy, time-manufacturer, that

remainder, murmuring bellflowers in votive sway.
        sometime all it need is a little shake.
        not this measure though.   next, maybe.
                            restless leg a lot.
        is that enamor escaping through his
            abscesses with every labored breath?

            mary lou, i'm sick. wonder can you help me?

spin out further and farther
            from searching and unarrive. repeat:

            dabble of keyboard, the most radiant
radials. anything that happened to him
went into his ears and came out of his fingers

étude op. 15, no. 3 (four for therapy)

aint no party like lean you carry around wherever you go, cuz lean swerve with outlawed. but loose is more around, became for him just an excuse of melody to be supple somewhere with her. it was, but then it. longing's tennessee whiskey coming through his pores. stale beer breath. come on in with brush for this head.

dry long so so long some ashy turned ash turned ache with bags under eyes for forgetting. hard liver. slump. drank all you want just leave some. can you put yourself in the other's position, prone and defenseless? there go the volleys, blows and kicks. organize it for sound.

grind all the anguish down on the piano. where things are meeting and complicating each other. notwithstanding: the struck-awe, the long extended assault in police custody was off the clock and a lazy sermon on white sunday. took that beat down for us. for to spend evenings rubbing us.

modern at a moment's notice, already various resolutions ahead. listen to her and watch her procure. funny thing: a rare velocity happened on the way to the playhouse. ride like an unopened-endec nascence. how luxuriant against high cheekbone going away.

un poco loco

What if the men of sense need to be
checked by the men who don't have
any?

FRED MOTEN

mnemonic fragments (ballad for crossing the unbridgeable chasm)

6. if you start in the middle of
the bridge, nobody knows
which way you are going,

7. only the acolytes and believers know there is no deity.

33.   everyone else tries to put you in restraints
                    because you crush and run through all provision.

18. *in a sentimental mood—*
hundreds of thousands of gallons of water per
second pouring over
the falls
crushes you like attendants come running.

51 a. sofas, tables, couches moving,
occassionals, loveseats, chairs in the air—
ring the nurses' desk. the sun
            gets loud in your eyes.
pick tears out of the air.

1. magnetics are drivers such as. there is
composition that goes.
then everything. do you understand why

2. you are here?

8. restless tapping
to distraction. either you have transmittal,
or you can't get out of the bag.

51 b.   the lab coats say,
what choice have you
            given them, but
to take your choices away.

20.   fragrance of harsh
flower. define crazy.

27. something else is going
                        on here,

28. am i the only one that can hear subtlety
in choking?

5. that *un* sound is coming
                over the ramparts.
            i don't think i'm acting strange.

19. does anybody have a cigarette? each manifests as a.

13. the chlorpromazine hollows
            you out.
tiny, dark pupiled eyes
on the edge of
a counter.

25.   become the bed
without visitors for weeks.
                a face divided, a clinic on fixation.

15. am i ever getting out of here?
                skiff of instruments tuning in my frontal.

52. what if
                    the diagnosis is a brownstone
        without an instance of hustle?

26. tragedies are a minor fraction of.

16. better to shit and cry than be happy.

53.   as a follow up
                question: how to play
        and delight your way through the diagnosis?

4. these delayed windows in entreaty. hard
to keep my wings together. racking.

17. why do i keep forgetting *you go to my head*?
and who else am i hiding from?

29. distant piano playing (itself?)

piano solitaire

so excited to be fingers again.
most fools aint even foolish enough to
          try to sit in when his gash is cooking.
the line all the way around the corner
come from georgia to kick you in your long tail.
whole damn tenement come together to
give him a ride to wherever he want.
he improvise off of them long loving
looks of all his aunties and play mamas,
display parlance he learn in packages.

sly how that wrong note is the right wrong note.
          the stick he always lending brake his head
in variations, only have to hear
it go up to know how it got back down.

earl of harlem at the golden shovel

in lush discord at the cogent ledge we
heard, *yeah, you can play the piano but where's your left
hand.* and it was follow along or get left at school.

head cocked back, left pant leg pulled up past the knee, we
are chewed lips as a side effect of chlorpromazine's lurk.

up and down the keyboard exhaustively of late,
a set of unavailable tones was all *mind ya business* when we
were inquisitive around when the keys went on strike
and refused to move even a quarter note straight
ahead. is it a fool's fancy or a wail? we
seek the unexpected in a subdominant realm to sing
the sweet score beyond threshold of sin.

the suffering is not difficult, but terrible to hear. we

try to keep him upright on the bench, but his blood is thin,
he has never really been able to hold his gin.

our fatha which art in stride, how are we
ever going to forgive his successes and let him just jazz?
for what can the cool days of autumn tell anyone about june?

everybody dancing a little impermanent dance as we
wring every ounce of cadence out of him. die
hard fans around the bandstand praying it ends soon.

the negro section as frontage

territorial adagio, zooted in the righteous quarter of if

        the left hand offends art tatum, you

better damn near cut it off. that wasn't

all moonlight and intimation in a minor key, but just
    enough blood to fill a slow bottom of love. cavort as

    a down pat lick dream of no city limits, happy
    is the ticklish mind. up-high birds take liberties to

tight spaces like back teeth. sun too fuzzy in the cold, gray sky to be

a significant player but nothing can stop it from getting down. here
    he damn go. every genius mutilates themselves on the one, as

the crowd is all tangential ears off on some commodified flight. forget you
      ever heard the wing break, his othered tune was
      better than a soft landing in some fatted sax to

upstairs where black folk are made to sit. deep guttural imaginings, come

    correct, he shows flexibility, flips it, then

the modernist feel for them fat-ass thighs. you know, what-

ever dude you brought to the session is long gone daddy. you

thought about them legs and that you was their ride home. it's gon'
    be hard travels and unlikely to the next station. to do what he do,
how he devastates, thump, a divergent maneuver folded in the simple

    smoke he built in like a contradiction, like a motherfucker.

he built in and not out to go all out because of a sense of smoke. the

relevant silt, the newer bend in the river turned gilead into a salve.
a scar to swoon, the devil deep up in it, ready to make a trade.

12-bar F blues with a few substitutions thrown in

the bootleggers take me through my paces,
as you follow along with me on a binge
on a lengthy bender. been a hot mic
since. energy doesn't lie. chew all
the fat around, low-slung elbow, wrists flat
as kansas. i got a right to outstretch,
i liked to got a killer stuck in a tree.
i see people dancing no one else sees.
they don't know they are unseen. to somehow
find time to arrive at conjectural
about a fitful compartment i hide
some stuff in: emotional distances,
ranging voices, needles, thirteen stairs down,
blood in my eyes, this wrong at the fastenings of it.

.

wor studios, new york city, may 1, 1951

blue note's little chain smoker
just outside.   long-ass ash, somewhere bereft of body.
who gonna call it in on the one
condition? a night air felt
between some roiling fingers. six sails of upper atmosphere
clouds with regards to not feeling the need to cop for a minute.
                                        cleaner than a cop's revolver
or his official record,
ready like freddy if he had just shot up.

over two hours late
when he finally dashed into the studio dapper,
a decade early, and a concert piano.

fast as it could go and still be contiguous.
so many little clusters
with contents that contain quivers
and their discontents.
the little clusters. to the tune gallery of
his curly hair on fire, circle back
to a tormented country. it was impossible
to convince him no one was knocking

on a windowpane after crusade,
or that there wasn't eventual beacon
for portal instead of a microphone.
thanks to a dedicated bottom,
despite tempests, he played through
a prescient gap-leggedness above the overdubs.
the sides got down and
bent the little improper platform till it
held all the space in everyone's heart.

tempus fugue-it

that rip-off was a riff off moonlight, an homage.
i thought all last night about her
not being here sempre dolce with me.
i liked to kill time like ted(dy),
and time flies when you're trying to kill flies
with a rolled-up *new yorker*. i never fathomed
                flies don't bleed
when i found what i later found out were scarlet
aspects of its guts smeared on pg. 63.
in most instances, the instant composition church
of (listening to those) cognitive hands for deviating around.
to the maniacal establishing deep ear sympathies,
to the oneiric fade in the way of things (in town),
to the black granite floor that does not give (a damn).

earl of harlem swear he in love with the little piano girl of east liberty (alternate take)

love is the piano playing for your fingers
   through circles of fifths in search for level eleven.
heart as an instrument of uncompromising pulse,
whatever gives off light must endure burning.

a circle of fifths in search of level eleven
is orchestra that send me integrally to solo.
whatever gives off light must endure burning
   passion invading from inside the inside.

inner orchestra send me integrally to solo,
riff, and venture farther toward center.
   passion is being invaded from inside,
as if to catch one's breath unfaithful to the heart.

riff and venture farther toward center.
slow your finger rolls against season of heartbreak.
as if to catch one's breath unfaithful to the heart,
   no way home save through these pangs.

slow your finger rolls against season of heartbreak.
got an upright baldwin piano for a heart
   that sees me through these pangs.
times you're left holding with luxuriant withholding.

   a small, upright baldwin piano for a heart
is an instrument of uncompromising pulse
for when you're left holding with luxuriant withholding.
   love is the piano playing for your fingers.

last supper of bop

March 4-5, 1955
Personnel:
Charlie Parker - Alto Saxophone
Kenny Dorham - Trumpet
Bud Powell - Piano
Charles Mingus - Bass
Art Blakey - Drums

iv.
the bandstand was tableland everybody gathered around
in the club where the piano wouldn't play anything.
a dealer is anxious to sell some fix to the saxophone
who doesn't want those kinds of extracurricular distractions.
at least not tonight, which he desperately needs to be a pathway
that leads expeditiously through this present down and out.

vii.
insistent clave, necktie crooked, socks inside out,
in no discernible shape to shape a chord around
a distal enclave. at one point, he got so sideways
you thought he was asleep at the keys. the next thing
you know tightly cuffed pant's leg get some kick drum action
going, and you would have thought the saxophone

iii.
would be back by now, but he's interceding at the bar
with another saxophone.
you could hear patience wearing thin, and welcome
                                    wearing out,
and the club's named after him, but you think he's getting
any of the action?

chaos was encircling and widening on the dais around
the piano's silent encampment against everything
ensemble, not unlike a breathless child determined
                        to get his way.

vi.
to get the dodge out of timbre in a way
that would be overture to the saxophone.

lint in his hair and on his suit, googly-eyes at everything,
the audience had a ball figuring the piano's theatrics out.

most had eschewed any hope he would come around
the bend and fly into his customary axial style of action.

ii.
for every axial, there is a coaxial and opposite reaction.
this D flat the bass had been making an expressway
for if the quintet ever came together around
a passage the little piano would get into with the sax.
but instead of trading eights, a melodic fight broke out,
resulting in the piano sneaking off to do his own thing

v.
down reluctant corridor. bird endeavored to blow something,
anything. the wheeze and clicking, suction, and pump action
of a brass lung was bright locomotion coming out
of a programmatic tunnel. it swept up the theoretical in
                  its outlying railway
and made it buoyant. this is the surgical work saxophones
do in extemporaneous suites. the toe-tapping around

i.
the venue subsided as more people looked around.
something ominous seemed to be out there in transaction
                  with the saxophone.
it wouldn't even be two weeks before bird flew far, far away.

mingus of the ninth circle

clouds of compositions in the interposed—gray-high till shiloh come. first,
here must be

uplifted
a bass,

somewhere of agile digits
the mystery, so

careful among the pleasures. she is brought to rhapsody comping

in her. stand open-valved. conception ajar.
is investigative daddy at the ninth circle,
third avenue

from crucial? gig-loot-filled socks. half-yaller coming forth,
the swing endless, yet

most things might as well not be there to most.
know that they are

there,   even if you don't know

long-bowed solo, a hymn

lined out, orgiastic, a sonata, duke, yeah. clairvoyant

bird rathers, *don't take that next out breath out
of context*, cause

excruciating is exploratory,
chordal terrain. a man is little looking out over the landscape
going home on the morning

four four.

oh, mingus,

so rough, so tough. arrogant   orchid

the portrait of an artist in his daughter's aural imagination

      i never met my father that early hour, he wandered off in the rain but didn't get wet because of the piano in him. a jaundiced smirk of moon. why concern the wind when it never remembers anyway? long before i was born he had escaped into a versicolor only one or two others could navigate. is there a point at which you no longer ask yourself but beg the muses instead? so many haggard and incomprehensible bars to far-flung. he would go to sleep, and the music would go into a little attention room he built with reddish-brown molding around the vaulted ceiling. piano lessons in his lap were inlaid and marvel. when he gets to the part with the two-finger javelins, he teaches me to launch myself into my sorrows with satchel. you can tell he does not know where he is going with me but can't admit it. i overhear a little girl out in front of the liquor store asking if her father is inside prefacing bartok. *he is not well. please, don't give him beer or money.* mornings humming "johnny angel" and cleaning up vomit beside his bed, glad it's not his cooling board. always barrelhousing nimbly up one side after brahms, and down the other side amok with fortissimo. i want an ending that is open-ended, but this is not one of those.

crash

                                                    depression above
embankment trees hide forest a car rolls into. automobile far across crush in carriage.
unless you know music,
                             you wouldn't know from the melody richie was dead. nancy and
                     clifford, too.

               state police call before daybreak disturbed birds singing.
a body in shock tremors.

pale light. dim bulb.

pearl dropped the phone into chasm, courageously reached back in   in hopes she heard
the confusion of traffic. but it was coast breaking from mainland. one of many black mornings.
couldn't get bud off the floor,

                        probably couldn't see her hands in front of her for the downpour.

            somehow the piano found him,
            wrapped its keys around him.   the island
                                                        was

            castaway man in this dirge crossing a sound in his grief.

homegoing and repass

i. way forward through

double doors. go

down in death. holp us

with her incandescent bones up
aisle. teeth

missing in preacher's mouth.

he might be able to relate.
listening

to mahaila singing

on back of fan.

mama rock with

the baby. elegy minor. rev

spoke more to the living

about dying, made that land

terrible and welcome.
organ worked on the balls of

feet. bass lead jumped all around
congregation backing

him up. so much shouting
police enjoyed it in their misprision.

this ain't none of my home. bud needs a
drank, but trying not to look like it.

everybody else sweating cause
it's hot as all get out in this church.

ii. oscar's and sons' placed bellflower,
lavender, and daisy reef outside the
door. to people in the community
that didn't know—a signal to ask
somebody. think bud cares it looks
like he's talking to himself. fold the
loss up into layers in pit of the
stomach. the kitchen is a full
circle.

with pies, cakes, ribs, fried chicken, and macaroni everyone come to
the setting up bud won't sit up at. holds his breath, swims under the
conversation. many try not to sit next to him for fear of catching
something, but they're taking up whole couch with incorrect posture
to him. pearl tired is everybody's auntie without giving a nod. things
more important than the quotidian call from alcove of his mind. he
won't be back for remainder.

iii. throw out so much
food only a few days after funeral.
grief is a life

sentence. so what
are you going to do?
waiting for richie to answer what time

it is, why the f is sharp, when is
he picking him up for the gig. sense
might not catch a break again.

solo

awhile the ensemble played the absence of her touch. hardly to the little boy wanting with the big eyes, unexpected for rows. about to lone crackle of light against the night and long for intimate sustain. waiting for the horn on some tips. that feeling feeling. wail-like. there go the bridge you can't kiss.

for every kiss the fingers missed. the sax talked you back where a breath is doing this so alone. the little boy wanting. come on up the road always watching and listening off to the side where nobody else is. this ensemble is one in the last chorus. that to come. after the gone is break

as a way to allow other space.

why doesn't the thunder roll me? then, silence. then,

a clarion sound in the body, a song back to. marrows all the various tones of alone and off to the side to yourself. not apart of,   just ache. and empty. and flute mint of crave. the very end played on.

70

paris spring, autumn in new york

You got to dig it to dig it, you dig?

THELONIOUS MONK

lost in the 8th arrondissement

and then it coheres,

or does it?

clouds thin to betray the oath

the moon swore.

      clouds

in search of further   periphery

---

with its pale

provenance however obliquely somewhere.

in a way that might be considered outlying, in another way

thought to be the other way, glancing over my left

shoulder

a lot i don't want to remember.

---

most of the time you are not where you are.

there are whims

at the tips.

if there are differences at all, it is in tone.

---

the curvature of staggering.   the answer is far too

much

    wild turkey.

that's regret you hear in the action

my head against the building makes.

loss hushed between us.

there goes a clearing

      with its vertices breaking

silence

come with me

then to no decision about any kind of discreet or timing

until we've found the owlishly up. do you know the

piece? the rain matters more when you barely speak

the language and are outside of it.

      blow

      it's always perpendicular lines that

the gentlest up,

    and district.

    flics are pigs.

      make the light heavy, uniform,

a hand on her heart for the taking.

    i guess i got a frame that doesn't

completely frame or takes too long to sharp.

    rue means away we go.

winter.

from house to abandoned house,

    it's difficult to see in or out.

    like a quality, just glad to see the back of this

earl of harlem on bob thompson's garden of music

bob put his foot in this one so deep, at first you can't hear the wild
blues ricocheting out the frame. before you
know it, his oculus is in you. he hit you with
that pentatonic phantasia, and you be fond of
feldspar and wanting that prodigious, ochre
stream filling you irreducibly with sentence. line
and color have you rethinking and dreaming the
way the waters are evidentiary and flow uptown
with him when he's got a seam too tight. the
picture is melodious. it gets hypodermic from
encampment, and without a countdown, the
orange tramp is a glorious dehiscence after
habit of scads. the other way out there are
churlish ovals of agonies. as now. then, like so
many junkies before fray, the shooting gallery
is the first day of the monterey jazz festival. you
see? when you gets a style you stole together,
you innovates without portion. prima facie
primitive, you say? salient reductivity in main?
my iris. the gouache is a study in bass and the
basest fears of
jonesing. that chroma tree is an abridged bridge. the brown boy thinks
he is his own dog rubbing his behind against an allegory
balsam. the drummer doesn't look right out of
his wife's clothes. but what i really want to know
is, how'd he mix his oils out of my subconscious?
he had to have put some water in the chord, but
made sure it was clean, so you could hear clear
through it. what's more, my fellow aesthete,
what's more chromatic than a broader interest
in technique than in representation? most of
our young colorists lack a feeling for melody, but
not ol' bob. he understands harmony is the basis
of the theory of color. his pigment is jamming
and doing all the showing in his storytelling. dig
the ambiguous spaces between vanguards on
their own terms. there are more questions than
answers in the denuded sextet of sensitivities.
alienation being front and off-center. now
that your wig is split like ol' girl's, you feel that
thought peeking from behind the mangrove in
her nude color chemise. off you go through the
yellow ambient trauma groves..

dissipation: a bop

                                    he's two-fisting it, there are overtones
                and tones under undertones to this,
                he lists from one side to the other sidecar, drops
                            of sweat tumbling down tumblers.
them tremblement de terres are how liquid
turns to brick in the belly. here we are

ba dabba dooba ba dabba dooba dabba
ba dabba dooba ba dabba dooba ba dabba doo ba da ba da ba dabba doo
ba dabba dooba ba dabba dooba ba dabba doo ba da ba da ba dabba doo
ba dabba doo ba daaa

                        again, belly up, already forgotten
the last time and working on forgetting
this one with out of focus,
eyes in the glass looking more in.
a marker of entertainment and leisure,
                        bruised pear is hard pressed to withhold.
                        bartender cut him off, but he sips from table
                        to table for a quick second, or third with any spirit.

ba dabba dooba ba dabba dooba dabba
ba dabba dooba ba dabba dooba ba dabba doo ba da ba da ba dabba doo
ba dabba dooba ba dabba dooba ba dabba doo ba da ba da ba dabba doo
ba dabba doo ba daaa

                        another bud for bud till there isn't any bud left.
                          where does this caravan pony up from all
unmitigated? and where does abandon arrive at?
                              no appetites only thirst.
                      a whiskey bar walks into a negro, staggers out
a piano talking about, *vin s'il vous plaît.*

ba dabba dooba ba dabba dooba dabba
ba dabba dooba ba dabba dooba ba dabba doo ba da ba da ba dabba doo
ba dabba dooba ba dabba dooba ba dabba doo ba da ba da ba dabba doo
ba dabba doo ba daaa

off night: a piano trio

where is the best place to wear a suit, if not while taking a bath? and why does a music stand make the best bedfellow despite its cold feet and sharp toes?

a nervous, nervously entered, upstairs.

crack in the vanity was feeling need to parlay a drink, when not a nip more was tenable. more and more often of several disagreeing minds of manic hammers showing up to the spot undone. go down moses's spilt spiked tea, a teaspoon used like tuning fork, a prickly specter, hide-and-go-seek underneath the piano, the other zero, not one, not (not) two, three sheets, all a jitter, the nether
of the fool

to fall through two sets late, too high to touch key. rickety scale, sprung ladder fractures somewhere half an octave up. splinters in fingertips, ascent split into eighths and fifths were canary flitting madly up and down on broken wing. this occasioned struggle of bass stumbling over the drums. that G flat tonic got off but forgot to resolve.

sometimes an
inattentive audience listens up
to discover they're in a ramshackle, hole-in-the-wall club with a hole in the wall from some policeman's fist, patched up and filled haphazardly with thirty-secondths interspersed with semitones, and nobody knows how the haints got loose, kicked in the bassdrum, broke the neck of the bass, knocked over the entire front row of tables and chairs till the promoter is so embarrassed he cuts his losses. tonight, sky is a lightless, bloodshot eye.

tomorrow, all hail—his highness, the earl of harlem will have missed the montmartre vineyards in spring from the hangover.

last call

been cold-sweating since the shaft and lovejoy slipped out. the burning sensation in the chest is the answer, but it's evil. within ninety seconds, the savages are untwisted, the walls padded. i stop seeing two times what everybody else sees.
stepping off it
makes me feel like i have butterflies in my fingertips. i said, *i am about to be brandy's bitch this evening*. all anybody could do afterwards was somehow help me back to my flat. intractable's

poor liver. too much to handle, too much is not even enough. not enough triads and block parties to fill the canyon, but enough to bridge across it. somebody like me flooded the bridge though.

you ever collar a blind fella?   what does control feel like?
a blade's sharpness is different coming at you. you won't stop it

if you think it's the cure. it tastes like slapping the taste out of an abusive cop's mouth, like baby's

first drops of mother's milk
until you tremble without it. then it tastes like a prescribed burn, such a lonely savor.

give me just one drink, but i will take as many as you pour.
stepping into it makes it hard to maintain.
i was

drunk when i dotted my own mama's eye.
i was drunk when the police knocked out
two teeth. i was drunk when god shook
both my hands in acknowledgment of my
evenhandedness. i was drunk when celia
was born. i was drunk when i signed the
contract, and goodstein didn't give a shit. i
was drunk if we were ever introduced.
years of hours being confined

to a concave mirror. the
hundreds of times i yawn and
toast jim crow between the
times when i have audience's
ears all pliant and solicitous
before my oracle. the need to
have some thoughts slowed.
nobody knows the double i
see. nobody knows what key
i'm in. laid out in a dank alley
between halibut guts, egg-
shells, and moldy potatoes,
between sleep and stupor with
dry heaves.
the sweet rot.
to project from the stomach
through the mouth with such
regularity. are the voices self-
talk or auditory? either way,
aint trying to hear it—with no
success.

fraternité

fra·ter·ni·té, /fʁa.tɛʁ.ni.te/, noun, from old french francis, as in, paudras, borrowed from latin frāternitās, frāternitātem, from frāter ("brother"). **1.** brotherhood: the state of being vigilant by his bedside at les hôpital, and constantly in the doctor's ear advocating for the black body. **2.** brotherhood: the state of bailing his black body out of la prison every time he is found drunk wandering des rues or passed out in la ruelle or la gouttière. **3.** brother's keeper, esp. when the neighbors complain, and gendarmerie shows up to the soirée, and instead of hassling him, have a brandy and flute or two before dancing out of the flat. **4a)** *brother, can you spare a courvoisier or take an axe to his light complected neck for him?* **b)** a deaf ear turned to delirium tremens talking. **c)** a being with his shivering black body, while ever so gently drying him out. **5.** after your pregnant wife goes to sleep you open up a sub rosa category nook of cherished eyes between you and him. **6.** secrets shared with you he would normally only whisper to the keys. **7.** an association or organization of men or boys, esp. cops after they have fractured the skull of his black body and crushed his orbital socket for what they all claim was a violent resistance to arrest. **8.** pigs, or the close tie among crooked cops that compels them to conceal crime in their ranks. **9.** three matadors, and a bleeding bull with flesh on his horns and six lances between his shoulders. **10.** two pond tortoises simultaneously break the surface of the water. **11.** several feathers wafting down from a perch.

aubade: earl of harlem composing extemporaneously

tones cluster
until the melody is quite a query,
quixotic encounter

between two intervals. inscrutable
overtones like a heart
is a beautiful hideaway. intervals as self

-portrait. noteworthy. note like
a chrysanthemum blossom bursting open.
unruly noted. like crazy little ideas

crawling all over the keys. unpredictable
semitone. you look sans partitions running
down the rue dauphine chasing notes.

the middle C was a complete sentence and a bird
flying away from a flock. promissory note. notes
that gaze at the male gaze. sound advice:

in every interval is an archive
you arrive at as strangers and leave abruptly fast friends.
no one heard that attack coming. the interval was a cry

for help from a lead sheet
bounded by dark flesh. note to black self to
behold your fungibility to white society. there comes

a time in a young black man's life
when you must establish the ground
you're walking on, as if to denote it,

you have to run in the opposite direction of the police
sirens; innocence be damned
and caught up with later like a chorus.

a sound you can better get away with in france.
A sharp as a needle
that can't find a vein, but that doesn't stop

the search. B flat so eager to trace and arc
around an early grave. estranged notes. high note
as a sycamore from its falling leaf's perspective. high note

more than two bottles of bordeaux in.
high notes of otherness. more notes to self.
did nutty fingers actually bet you a c note?

a wigged out note, flat out? out
past paris proper, humming
a little ahead? was the break

a dawn? a G major as a kind of fog-belted clearing
in the 'fore day morning waiting to warm.
F sharp like sunup is a loud popping of light.

a regatta of triple triads perfectly mishapes
a pinkish-orange horizon darkly bulged with notes
of purples, a genius of distance every so often noted.

gigan: epistle to neptune

the contours within the breaks, auricular to the point
of being a five-note anemone to end the second

phrase going inward like breath circling—dear desire to
drown myself every day, dearest king neptune, you can't do me
no harm like light fingers of moon on the water for sound-

check: where is the piano in the sea? taken to the water
a tone more varied inward searching mute going inward, deeper

than a bite, this deep, in the deep, explore how deep
is lowdown and what color is bottom. that curved timing

is sexy on the boundaries and giving the left the right to conjure. the fingers
find and break the contours by ear, concord sharpens the point.

took a pint with me to the water where the piano is in the sea,
laid out, and baptized my subconsciousnesses tightly together
in nuances. now, none but the righteous shall. now, hush sweetly

these other waters, in essence, horizon note, clarity dance of magnificent
ocean depths, epitome in discrete blue, that interval. up out, earl of harlem.

blue heron

i.

unfixes the eyes, sends them asking
among the ripples of its wake
for it, for even a silhouette, if it was
anything. if it can be more than just
heard, but known, notated. the
shoulders unaccustomed to holding
up this much uncertainty, shrug. the
far resonance, the fortuity. that to
carry you where you curve
perpetually forward.

ii

was awaiting the wind, whether it
would say whether, or not. wouldn't
even say if, either way. crosswinds.
took the semitone right out of the
air, moved through it echoic, and
alary it descended a vessel of
solemn

iv.

for estuary. the ostinato of
headwaters. dream meaning river.
the six rivers run home. upstream,
the almost light in the distance, a
body of smoke on its way away. that
just barely audible, repeatedly wing.
whispered offering up. and this
gone is a tonic above. attention

celia

in the latter years, when your father plays the piano for beers, your memories of him
are thin and impressionistic. you call him mercurial and recall him mostly when
other people mention him. it doesn't help that he is infamous.

*

one day after a lifetime of self-exile, he came home clean and sober from paris with gifts. it
wasn't long before he broke the brake pedal again.
seventeen candles light the disappointment in a girl's face. the young girl's eyes reading
him her rights.

*

the next day, i saw this man stagger into my room, pull out my chester drawer, turn around,
sit down, and urinate on my underclothes.

*

i know it's hard when you inhabit the lawless space between the laws of music
and the laws of meaning, but every excuse can't be that you are barely alive between
performance.

*

the next day everything was blanketed with snow; he was admitted,
and what it sounded like was inextricably connected to how you feel
all alone with no heat and no money to pay the bill.

*

sometimes icicles, sometimes everything seems adrift.
this remorse was among the softest tenors in my father's repertoire:
its florid fills and their minor colors sent me.
i am here,

i want to say *bel suono* but can only summon distant.

*

of course, he fit an insane number of notes in a half of a chorus, he was crazy, and sensitive
on top of self-medicated, on top of no respecter of boundaries.

*

a heart instrument, his piano weighed a ton.
everybody and everything in the room,
even the walls, were mesmerized by his fingers.
they had their own personalities, unique qualities.
and his fingering had a distinct character, it wasn't just acuity or rapidity, it was how it
got around to being its own voice for changes.

*

o, the changes.
one day you get a fresh direction with each new day,
and it seems the more expansive your ear becomes the more agency you forfeit,
and it's in this valence, deep in the tissue of your knowing that
a strange father you're estranged from fades out of garment into breezeways.

appendix

To her [Mary Lou Williams], every
bop pianist after Bud Powell played
Bud Powell.

LINDA DAHL

notes

The fret is a poetic form invented by Mitchell L. H. Douglas. Visually, the poem is supposed to suggest the appearance of the fretwork on a guitar with the two vertical black lines disrupting the lines and syntactical flow of the poem like line or stanza breaks. The first letter of the first word that begins each line of the poem corresponds to the note in the fret. "blues in b for Charlie," "riff on g7," and "mad man at the finger palace (alternate take)" are examples of this form in this collection.

In "blues in b for charlie," we have an homage to electric guitar pioneer and Bebop founder Charlie Christian. Christian, along with Thelonious Monk, Kenny Clarke, Mary Lou Williams, Dizzy Gillespie, and Charlie Parker, is considered by most scholars to be one of first purveyors of Bebop or Bop. In this poem, we have one of the first of many referencing to cutting or cutting contests, which was artists playing the same instrument competing to outplay one another bar for bar, note for note. The "cutting" could take place in many forms and contexts. (See trading eights and rent party.) Bob Johnson is a reference to the legendary Blues guitarist Robert Johnson. Reportedly, Charlie Christian and Robert Johnson had a cutting contest once in a juke joint outside Memphis, and Christian played circles around the Blues legend. There is an old carpenter's maxim: "measure twice, cut once," which is referred to in this poem.

Earl "Bud" Powell, Thelonious Monk, Elmo Hope, and Al Walker were all close friends, pianists, and early innovators of Bebop. They hung out in the early 1940s teaching each other music theory, blues riffs, and chord changes. Of the four, Al Walker was the only one who was not a full-time musician. He ran a TV repair shop to supplement his income, and the friends hung out in the backroom where Al kept a piano for them to play around on and teach each other their musical ideas.

Mary Lou Williams is the most important and well-known Jazz composer, arranger, and pianist that people do not know about. Williams's career spanned some sixty years. She saw all the changes in the art form and is arguably the only musician that changed with the music. Always forward-thinking, Williams's Harlem apartment was legendary for the artistic, intellectual, and political salons she hosted there. Williams's Sugar Hill apartment and Minton's Playhouse, more than any other spaces, lay claim to the "birthplace of Bebop." Duke Ellington said of Williams: "[she] is perpetually contemporary. Her writing and performing have always been a little ahead throughout her career. Her music retains, and maintains, a standard of quality that is timeless. She is like soul on soul." Williams was still in elementary school when her professional music career began. She played small concerts and was the featured artist at events and parties held at the homes of wealthy white patrons in Pittsburgh, PA. She was a child prodigy and given the moniker "little piano girl of East Liberty." The triad of pantoums that reference this nickname in the title were created with JavaScript. The first and last poems underwent heavy editing, while the middle poem was written with a small edit to the program to create the sentence fragments with very little editing on my part.

The alternate take is a poetic modality invented by Mitchell L. H. Douglas in which the alternate versions of poems present new information and interpretations of the original poems. In the iterations of this form in the collection, the original poem and its alternate(s) share a great deal of the same language and diction.

The reference to Igor Stravinsky is not because I am fond of him or his music. His well-documented anti-semitism and misogyny are nonstarters for me. I reference him here because his music was appreciated and studied by Jazz musicians of this time period who slipped passages from his repertoire and that of other classical composers into their compositions and improvisations..

"Jesus," "Bud," and "Earl of Harlem" were some of Powell's many nicknames. "High Priest of Bebop" was one of Monk's many nicknames. Monk was famous for wearing a wide variety of interesting hats. Powell's idol and mentor, pianist Art Tatum, was nicknamed "God" for his virtuosity on the piano. After Tatum died, some in the NYC Jazz community began referring to Powell as "God."

A rent party was a social occasion where tenants hired a musician or band to play and pass the hat to raise money to pay their rent, originating in Harlem during the 1920s. The rent party played a major role in the development of Jazz and Blues music and was often the location of cutting contests.

Humoresques is a piano cycle by the Czech composer Antonín Dvořák. The "Tiger Rag" is a Jazz standard that was recorded and copyrighted by the Original Dixieland Jass Band in 1917. It is one of the most recorded Jazz compositions. James P. Johnson, Fats Waller, Earl "Fatha" Hines, Willie "the Lion" Smith were all important stride pianists that exerted a great deal of influence on the styles of Monk and Powell. Pabst Blue Ribbon beer was Art Tatum's drink of choice. He would play the piano all night, and drink so many pitchers of Pabst that people would lose count.

The Gigan is a poetic form invented by poet Ruth Ellen Kocher inspired by the Japanese monster movie, *Godzilla vs. Gigan*. Gigan was low-budget monster that was made from the remains of Godzilla's vanquished opponents. The form consists of sixteen lines, includes five couplets and two tercets [in this order: couplet, tercet, couplet, couplet, couplet, tercet, couplet], with line one repeating as line eleven and line six repeating as line twelve.

Clark Monroe's Uptown House, sometimes shortened to Monroe's Uptown House or simply Monroe's, was a nightclub in Harlem. Along with Minton's Playhouse, it was one of the two principal clubs in the early history of bebop. The sonics in the poem "leit[blue]motif" *(duh-dun duh-dun duh-dun dun/ duh doobie doobie doobie doobie dudn doobie do do)* is a reference to the melody of Monk's tune "Light Blue." Sonics is a term that refers to the phonetic rendering of music in a work of literature.

The syncopated sonnet is a poetic form invented by Tyehimba Jess. It is a fourteen-line contrapuntal sonnet. The left half of the sonnet tells one side of a story, the right half of the sonnet tells a different side of that story, and you get the whole story when you read the lines straight across the page. "cutting contest: earl of harlem vs. art tatum (for who buys the next pitcher of pabst) (lost live recording)" is the only example of this form in this volume.

A cabaret card was a permit to work required of all labor, including performers, in New York City establishments serving alcohol from Prohibition to 1967.

The sonics in the poem "mad man at the finger palace" is a reference to the melody of Powell's tune "Un Poco Loco."

ECT is short for electroconvulsive therapy, a procedure done under general anesthesia, in which small electric currents are passed through the brain, intentionally triggering a brief seizure.

Trading eights refers to musicians alternating brief solos of pre-set length (the number refers to the number of bars played; 4, 8, and 12 were the most common bar lengths) in a call and response fashion. This trading usually occurs after each musician has had a chance to play a solo. It was also the structure used in cutting contests.

"tune as an asylum," "the negro section as frontage," and "earl of harlem at the golden shovel" are examples of the Golden Shovel poetic form invented by Terrance Hayes in homage to Gwendolyn Brooks. The last words of each line in a Golden Shovel poem are, in order, words from a line or lines taken often, but not invariably, from a Brooks's poem.

In Jazz and Classical musics, études are short musical compositions, typically for one instrument, designed as an exercise to improve a technique or demonstrate the skill of the player. My études consist of different instructions for each opus to assist the poet in developing her skills in creating, for example, nonrepresentational imagery or in verbing nouns in poems. Most études do not work as musical compositions. They are too theoretical, extremely challenging to play, and often not very musical because they are repetitions of a technique. Similarly, many of my études may not work as poems, because of the constraint of exercising a specific poetic device or move, but they will build the poet's skill in working with the nonconventional poetic craft elements that I am interested in, obfuscated metaphor and parataxis, for example. My études are divided into opuses. Each opus has a different set of instructions (prompts) or rules (many readers have suggested that the rules themselves are poems in the spirit of "recipe" or "spell" poems) to assist the poet in developing her desired skills. Each opus can produce an unlimited number of poems. The idea behind the études in this volume is these are pieces Powell composed on a piano he had drawn in chalk on the wall while deprived of a physical piano in the mental hospital. Powell created these études to practice and even expand his "chops" while he didn't have a piano and couldn't gig and perform on an almost nightly basis as he was accustomed to. I imagined this all taking place in the mental institution in a fictitious suite 120.

"the negro section as frontage" is a Golden Shovel based on the last sentence of Fred Moten's "the salve trade." "if you wasn't just as happy to be here as you was / to come then what you gon' do, simple motherfucker? the salve trade." From *hughson's tavern* (Leon Works). Copyright © 2008 by Fred Moten.

Common street names for heroin: horse, skag, smack, black tar, china white, dope.

Celia Powell was born Cecelia June Powell in 1948 to Bud Powell and his girlfriend Mary Frances Barnes. Although hospitalized, Powell had insisted that Barnes name the child for the patron saint of music. She was Powell's only biological child. He composed a famous ballad, "Celia," named after her. She passed away in 2009.

From the Academy of American Poets' website: "Not unlike the Shakespearean sonnet in trajectory, the Bop is a form of poetic argument consisting of three stanzas, each stanza followed by a repeated line, or refrain, and each undertaking a different purpose in the overall argument of the poem. The first stanza (six lines long) states the problem, and the second stanza (eight lines long) explores or expands upon the problem. If there is a resolution to the problem, the third stanza (six lines long) finds it."

The sonics in the poem "dissipation: a bop" is a reference to the melody of Monk's tune "Straight No Chaser."

Francis Paudras (b. 1935–1997) was a French commercial artist, author, and amateur musician. He was best known for his patronage and close friendship with Bud Powell, while the latter lived in Europe from 1959-1963.

acknowledgments

Thanks to the following journals and magazines for previously publishing poems in this collection:

32 Poems, ANMLY, Burzakh Magazine, The Bookends Review, Duende, Foundry, Harbor Review, Heart Journal, io Literary Journal, Killens Review of Arts & Letters, Literary Accents, lockjaw, North American Review, Prairie Schooner, Protean Magazine, and *Third Point Press.*

And without a doubt, I owe people. A lot of people. This list only mentions a few. If you were left out, charge it to my head and not to my heart.

These people have poured so much into me it is difficult to distinguish myself from them in me: Frank X. Walker, first and foremost. Ricardo Nazario-Colón, Randall Horton, Thomas R. Murray.

A very special thanks to Kyle "the poem-whisperer" Coma-Thompson for his close reading, exquisite edits, and full-throated support of this collection of poems when they really needed to hear it.

I am deeply indebted to my fellow Affrilachian Poets for our precious fellowship.

I am so thankful for these friendships: Josh English, Ron Davis, Chris Mattingly, Sonja DeVries, A. H. Jerriod Avant, and Jeremy Clark.

I would be remiss if I did not shout out all the Black women writers whose work more than anyone else's informs mine: Ruth Ellen Kocher, francine j. harris, DaMaris B. Hill, Lillian-Yvonne Bertram, Evie Shockley, Yona Harvey, Kiki Petrosino, Claudia Rankine, CM Burroughs, Airea D. Matthews, and Khadijah Queen. My highest aspiration is to be seen as a student of your work.

Lastly, I must acknowledge my enduring gratitude to the Cave Canem Foundation for creating a home for Black poetry that nurtures me every day on this journey.

PHOTO CREDIT: ANDRE HOWARD

makalani bandele is an Affrilachian poet and Cave Canem fellow. He has also received fellowships from the Kentucky Arts Council, Millay Colony, and Vermont Studio Center. He is a graduate of the University of Notre Dame with a BA in the Program of Liberal Studies, as well as a graduate of Shaw University with a Master of Divinity in Biblical Studies. He currently attends the University of Kentucky in pursuit of an MFA in Creative Writing. His work has been published in several anthologies, and widely in print and online journals, *African-American Review*, *Killens Review of Arts and Letters*, and *Sou'wester* to name a few. His collection of poems *hellfightin'*, his only other full-length work, was published by Willow Books/Aquarius Press in 2011.

New and Forthcoming Releases

under the aegis of a winged mind by makalani bandele
Winner of the 2019 Autumn House Poetry Prize
selected by Cornelius Eady

Circle / Square by T. J. McLemore
Winner of the 2019 Autumn House Chapbook Prize
selected by Gerry LaFemina

Hallelujah Station and Other Stories by M. Randal O'Wain

Grimoire by Cherene Sherrard

Further News of Defeat: Stories by Michael X. Wang
Winner of the 2019 Autumn House Fiction Prize
selected by Aimee Bender

Skull Cathedral: A Vestigial Anatomy by Melissa Wiley
Winner of the 2019 Autumn House Nonfiction Prize
selected by Paul Lisicky

No One Leaves the World Unhurt by John Foy
Winner of the 2020 Donald Justice Prize
selected by J. Allyn Rosser

In the Antarctic Circle by Dennis James Sweeney
Winner of the 2020 Autumn House Rising Writer Prize
selected by Yona Harvey

Creep Love by Michael Walsh

The Dream Women Called by Lori Wilson

AUTUMN
HOUSE PRESS

For our full catalog please visit: http://www.autumnhouse.org